Think & Grow

RISS

My Darling Soldier Girl

by Brian Wood

A Father, Daughter & Nana's Military Journey.

A father's recollections of a true story embellished with Platoon Nana poems.

"A Burning Desire Backed
by Persistence Does
Not Recognize Failure."

B. Wood

Copyright © 2023 Brian Wood

All rights reserved.

ISBN: 9798397861328
Imprint: Independently published

DEDICATION

To my father Colburn, who inspired and encouraged me through every significant and trivial accomplishment in my life. He was a genuine patriot. He was a man of faith who led and taught by example. The greatest compliment I could be paid would be "The fruit doesn't fall far from the tree."
1938 - 2021

To my son Michael, a staunch military supporter. He is a charismatic, strong and compassionate man. I am reminded daily there is no greater gift than one that comes with fatherhood.

Photos from a visit to Fort Hood
Army Base in Killeen, Texas

My Darling Soldier Girl

Contents

Each Chapter is a Recollection

The Inspiration 1
My Darling Soldier Girl 5
The Announcement 6
I Saw a Soldier Go to War 11
The Journey Begins Lee Greenwood 12
Red, White and You 17
God and Country 18
Dog Tags and Crosse 20
The Going Away Party 22
Through The Eyes of a Child 23
What To Give and Keep 29
MEPS - Reality Sets In 30
You Will Not Go Alone 33
Dreaded Boot Camp 34
Pretty Little Feet 37
Glasses vs. Glasses 38
Platoon Nana's in The Camp 40
Hey Guys 44
Artillery Training 45
My Wish 49
The DMZ - Demilitarization Zone 50
Excerpt from the song "We're More Alike Than Not" 52

Hold On Another Day 54
Fort Hood 55
Pink Ribbons 58
Two Years Have Passed 59
You Don't March Alone 62
Off to Kuwait - Fox Treats 63
God Only Knows 68
America's Heroes Are Home 69
Not All Returned 74
Let This Cup Pass from Me 76
His Brother's Carried His Body 77
Never Quit 78
Vets Continue to Serve 80
Road to the Honor Guard 81
Eternal Thanks 83
Freedom To Think - Democracy 84
Freedom Isn't Free 86
Americans measure the cost of war… 87
The Debt We Can Never Repay 88
The Debt We Can Never Repay 90
Behold The Freedom Tower 91
Freedom Tower 93
Thank You for Your Service 94
Thank You for Your Service 96
One in the Spirit 101

The Introduction

I hope that the time you take to read my story will reaffirm and reignite the spirit of patriotism we share as Americans. It is my desire that the recount of my journey will articulate the passion and conviction with which I boarded the roller coaster with my darling soldier girl. For clarification, my daughter Larissa is known to friends and family as "Riss." Hopefully, through my recollections and the poetry of Larissa's grandmother, Platoon Nana, you will gain insight into the journey of a typical fledgling soldier. Whether or not a soldier sets foot on a battlefield, they become American heroes on the day they take the oath of enlistment.

We all hope and pray there will never be another war. Unfortunately, this world is not Utopia. The evil, in the hearts of self-serving dictators, results in resentment and oftentimes mere jealousy; despots who covet our precious land, our intellectual properties and our natural resources. They envy our status among world leaders. They lose sight of the fact that the spirit of nationalism they crave is reserved for those who adopt and support democracy. We are a nation that cares. We are a nation that shares.

Think and Grow "RISS"
My Darling Soldier Girl

The dual title of my book was inspired by a dream that awakened me with a vivid thought of "Think and Grow Soldier" reeling in my mind. The night before I was searching my phone for a specific picture of Larissa (RISS). She was about four years old, dressed in full camo, hat and all. Surprisingly, no one in the family can recollect that outfit. It was definitely not a Halloween costume. Where did it come from? It must be destiny! I knew it was the perfect image to grace the cover of my book, originally titled, simply, "My Darling Soldier Girl."

   I then stumbled across other pictures of her in uniform, in her late teens and early twenties. It must have triggered something in my subconscious. Had you read the book "Think and Grow Rich" by Napoleon Hill, you would understand the context of riches. Larissa defined her riches. Her riches were to serve her country. I fell back asleep and woke up shortly after with "Think and Grow Riss" burning on my brain. So, rather than abandon the original title, inspired by my mother's poem, I chose to incorporate the play on words with My Darling Soldier Girl.

Carol Wood at Brian's Gallery on Wolf Street in Syracuse. She has been sending letters and poems to her granddaughter, Pfc. Larissa Wood, and the platoon at Fort Hood, where she's been dubbed "Platoon Nana." (David Lassman/dlassman@syracuse.com)

Platoon Nana

Local woman writes poems of hope to the soldiers in her granddaughter's platoon

By Dave Tobin
dtobin@syracuse.com

Carol Wood was worried. Her granddaughter, Larissa Wood, hadn't told her family she was joining the Army until she had. So Carol Wood did the one thing she thought might help them both. She put pen to paper and wrote — letters and poems. And she mailed them to Larissa at basic training at Ft. Leonard Wood, Mo.

It surprised Larissa when she received the first of her grandmother's letters. She didn't know she could get mail while in basic training.

Carol Wood kept sending them at least once a week. Often she included a poem. Larissa began reading them to her fellow soldiers. Amid basic training's demands and deprivations during one of the hottest summers on record, Carol Wood's letters and poems brought relief.

"They were really heartfelt," said Larissa, now a private first class at Fort Hood, Texas. "You have to go through so much more to send out a letter than you do to send a text message. It has that heartfelt sense behind it."

The Woods are from the town of Clay. Larissa, 20, is a Liverpool High School graduate. She attended Onondaga Community College for a semester before enlisting in the Army in May of 2011.

She joined the Army because she needed "something more exciting," she said in a text. "I needed a fast change." She works as a crew member in an Avenger air defense artillery team.

Carol Wood, 69, owned and ran Carol's Antiques Art & Gifts, which had its last location on 7th North Street. She now helps her son, Brian Wood, who is Larissa's father, at his Syracuse frame shop on the corner of Wolf and Salina streets.

POEMS, PAGE A-6

HOLD ON ANOTHER DAY

*At times the hopeless feeling
May seem more than you can bear
In the darkness of your anguish
You can't see the ones who care.*

The full version as well as other poems can be seen at media.syracuse.com/news/other/nannapoems.pdf

A childhood photo of Pfc. Larissa Wood at age 4 or 5.

The Syracuse Herald-Journal

Chapter 1

The Inspiration

The stars aligned and the inspiration for my story began the day before Veterans Day 2015. Platoon Nana was on the program to speak at the Veterans Day Event at the War Memorial in Syracuse, New York. My daughter Larissa was scheduled to come home in just two weeks.

I'll never fully understand what caused the raw emotions to spill from my heart and onto my iPad; five years of pent-up emotions released like a tidal wave. As fast I could think, I fed the iPad my buried and suppressed thoughts. Apprehensive of the tablet that I seldom used, my greatest fear was that the "antichrist of technology" would relegate my thoughts into a black hole. One push of the wrong button and my list of chronological events would be gone forever. Thankfully, I was able to save the outline that I originally titled "Something's Missing…My Darling Soldier Girl."

Throughout the book I will periodically refer to Larissa's grandmother as Platoon Nana; a term of endearment bequeathed to her by Larissa's boot camp platoon. I couldn't be prouder of my daughter and my mother; two of the most powerful women in my life.

Without Nana there would be no Larissa. Without "Riss" there would be no Platoon Nana.

I was remembering all the wonderful accomplishments my mother had achieved over the past five years; the songs, the poems, the meetings and all of the speaking engagements. I recognized her innate ability to convey thoughts and impart wisdom. I couldn't wait to hand off my draft and outline to platoon nana. Who better to craft the story of "My Darling Soldier Girl."

I am not a writer. My mother is the writer in our family, so I wondered what she would do with it. Her response was swift and final. She said what most wise mothers would say to their son, "this is YOUR story, not mine." And darn it, mothers are always right! So, here we go.... even though the non-writer is writing, this is as much about the "writer" that our military supporters refer to as Platoon Nana. I'm proud to call her mom.

This would probably be a good place to interject the fact that although the writer, Nana does not type. It was my father who transposed every word and thought onto paper. Without complaining he preserved the "hen scratching" of every poem, letter, speech and correspondence that she wrote.

Enjoy the original poems, excerpts of lyrics, snippets and "Nana-isms" sprinkled throughout the book. They are intended to inspire a deeper appreciation for our men and women in uniform.

Larissa's decision to join the Army had set us all on a new path; a path potentially filled with danger. Nana wisely observed and noted that it is more rewarding to take the road less traveled than the path of least resistance.

Nana coined the phrase

"Better the road less traveled than the path of least resistance"

The entire book and collection of poems is a testament to the power of turning apprehension into direction. Nana would challenge readers to critique each poem by the "heart" of poetry rather than the "art" of poetry.

Platoon Nana's poem "My Darling Soldier Girl" is the inspiration for everything that follows.

My Darling Soldier Girl

My Darling Soldier Girl
Is a source of pride and joy
She marches with the best of them
Keeps up with soldier boys.

My Darling Soldier Girl
Loves country, friends and family
She's capable and confident
There's nothing she can't be.

My Darling Soldier Girl
Reaches for the moon and sky
She's bright and brave and beautiful,
There's nothing she won't try.

My Darling Soldier Girl
Is so strong, yet gentle too.
There's nothing in this world
That my soldier girl can't do.

© Carol Wood

Chapter 2

The Announcement

Nearly 13 years ago on the day Larissa announced she joined the US Army, I was shocked. In retrospect I shouldn't have been so surprised.

Larissa came home from college and says to me "Dad, I joined the Army."
I didn't know how to respond. Have you thought about this? I asked.
Have you considered other branches of the military; Air Force, Navy, Coast Guard?
The army and the marines are notoriously boots on the ground. Men significantly outnumber women and we are at war.

I was a single father and my only daughter

decided to join the army while we were engaged in a war in Afghanistan. It's nearly impossible to convey the wave of emotions I was processing.

She had already made her decision and was working out and training at the recruiting office in Mattydale in preparation for boot camp. What does any good father do? You Got it. I had to accept Larissa's decision and support her one hundred percent. We are now a military family.

Larissa's mother's side of the family had a proud history of military service. Her grandfather served in the Korean War. Two of her uncles served as well. Though proud and conditioned to the military regimen, I'm sure they were equally concerned.

My pride was not diminished despite the fact that our family experienced a generational gap in service. My pride was exceeded only by my apprehension.

My grandfather and uncle were in the military. Because neither of my parents served, I never gave much thought to enlisting. I consider myself blessed that the years I was in my late teens our country was not at war. There was no threat of war.

I was young, newly married and in 1989 we had our son Michael. Larissa was born in 1992. I was in my early twenties when I started my own business. We purchased our first home, "a handyman special" and worked like dogs just to make ends meet. The military was the last thing on my mind. Now, it's first and foremost.

I always considered myself a brave guy. I trained in karate, rode motocross, participated in BB gun fights in the woods, painful apple fights at the "Haunted House" and on top of that had two strong, coordinated older brothers who toughened me up. I thought I was fearless, until now. What's different? Now, I'm a single dad and my only daughter is off to war. I was beyond scared. I was petrified. I was proud, yet petrified. Fear of war was certainly my greatest concern. What will she witness; a fellow soldier wounded or killed in her presence. Would she suffer physical wounds or experience mental trauma? Will she be forced to kill? The scenario looming largest in my mind, the possibility, God forbid, that she would not return.

I managed to suppress the worst-case scenario. Reality leaves me little consolation. My beautiful soldier girl is 5' 8" with blonde hair and blue eyes. She will be living in fields and on military bases with a predominantly male population, none of which left their testosterone at home.

This is crazy. Our lives are forever changed. We are now faced with the biggest challenge of all. Who will tell Nana. You can quadruple my emotions. Mom's the most empathetic person I know. She coined the simple yet poignant phrase: "Sympathy Ignites Us, Empathy Propels Us." She literally feels other people's pain.

Sympathy Ignites Us...
Empathy Propels Us.

Carol Wood

Nana in Retrospect

The year was 1968

My brothers and I were asleep upstairs. The evening news always included documentaries and accounts of the Vietnam War. Nana watched footage of soldiers shipping off, saying their goodbyes to wives, sweethearts, children, mothers and families. She thanked God her babies were too young to go, then sat at the kitchen table and penned "I saw a soldier go to war".

How times have changed. The fourth verse of her poem is now history; no exemption for wishing your baby a girl.

A generation later nana is sitting in an induction ceremony with her darling soldier girl in Syracuse, NY

I Saw a Soldier Go to War

1968 -In the midst of Vietnam War

I saw a soldier go to war.
A sight I'd never seen before;
'Nor ever want to see again,
As memory's eye recalls the pain.

I watched a soldier kiss his bride,
He fought to trap the tears inside.
I heard him vow that he'd be home
As she sobbed, "I couldn't live alone."

I saw a soldier kiss his child,
He swore he'd just be gone a while;
"Take care of mommy while I'm gone
and very soon I'll be back home."

I saw a mother kiss her son
She wondered where it had begun;
This dreadful war that claimed her world,
And made her wish her babe a girl.

© Carol Wood

Chapter 3

The Journey Begins
Lee Greenwood

Anyone that knows me will tell you that I have always been a huge believer in the law of attraction, setting goals and believing in something so strongly that your mind will attract it. I actually bribed my kids with a crisp "Andrew Jackson" to read the book "Think and Grow Rich" by Napoleon Hill. I wanted them to grasp this important fundamental; the relevance of positive thinking and setting goals.

Flash forward. On the spur of the moment, Larissa and I decided to vacation in Tennessee before she was shipped off to boot camp.

Fortunately, my best friend owns a log cabin in the mountains of Tennessee between Gatlinburg and Pigeon Forge. Perfect! Thanks to Jeff and his wife Lisa, it's affordable. There is no end to the list of "crazy" things to do; Dollywood Amusement Park, radical go-kart tracks, whitewater rafting, great restaurants, tourist attractions, talent shows and best of all, it's possible to make the drive in just one day. Gatlinburg, Tennessee is only twelve hours from Syracuse.

On an early Wednesday morning, we loaded my white MKS and headed for the hills. What's a long trip without good music? Lee Greenwood to the rescue; one of my favorite CDs, with one of Larissa's favorite songs. If you have ears, you have probably heard "God Bless the USA."

With the radio blasting on high, Larissa, her friends and I would sing that song at the top of our lungs, off pitch and in every key imaginable. Today was no different. Larissa blared that song every hour on the hour. At the end of twelve hours the competition for highest decibel ended in a dead heat.

It was getting late. We were exhausted but made the decision to "soldier on." We can make it to the cabin tonight. We kept each other company and stayed awake listening to music. Needless to say, we listened to Lee Greenwood's "God Bless the USA" at least a dozen times. Let's say 13 for the record. Lol...that was my grandmother's lucky number.

We rolled into Pigeon Forge close to midnight. It was dark. We were dog tired. Most of the town was asleep. As we rounded the bend, we were hit with bright lights flashing.

For a moment I wondered if we were in Las Vegas or Pigeon Forge. No signs like that in Syracuse; way too many sign restrictions.

In front of The Smith Family Dinner Theatre loomed the prophetic words LEE GREENWOOD LIVE IN CONCERT. Piercing the midnight sky, a thirty-foot neon testament to the law of attraction. Lee Greenwood is in Pigeon Forge. So are we.

The next morning on the drive to whitewater rafting, I called the Smith Family Dinner Theater and scored 2 tickets fairly close to the front where we could enjoy a nice dinner and take in the show.

I was thrilled that she was excited to go. Lee was the artist of my generation. Larissa's regard for

Lee pretty much hinged on her love of that one song in his repertoire.

We're on a roll, a second law of attraction is about to unfold. While we were in the holding area waiting to enter the theater, I excused myself and snuck away to ask the ladies working the ticket counter if there was a way to get a message to Lee. They tactfully and quietly instructed me to write a note that they would attempt to get to him. I wrote a message and hoped for the best. Sure enough, the message found its way.

Lee Greenwood asked if there's a Larissa Wood in the audience, if so, would she please stand. What an honor! Lee Greenwood read the original note to the audience. Everyone knew about the

"Padre" and "Pooh Bear"

twelve-hour long marathon his song inspired and that she was headed for boot camp. He interjected her into the rest of the concert and dedicated every military song to her.

Following the show, true to American patriotism, the audience greeted her and shared words of encouragement and appreciation. It was a proud moment for both of us. I could see her humility give way to pride. What a beautiful gift bestowed by strangers.

This concert will go down as my most memorable. What are the odds that it was videotaped and available for purchase?

Pretty good when you practice positive thinking. The video later proved to be the highlight of Larissa's going away party.

Our flag, the symbol of America's freedom, encompasses all who served to protect it

Red, White and You

A salute to our military

Stars and stripes forever,
It's a phrase that we've all heard
The images we conjure
From a gang of simple words.

I see the stripes of red and white,
The stars set off by blue.
"Old Glory" waving in the wind,
I see red, white and you.

I see our fathers and our sons,
Our daughters standing tall,
I see our bravest and our best,
Who heard our country call

Each day I'll raise our precious flag
With reverence all anew
I'll see her symbols and her colors,
But mostly…I'll see you

© Carol Wood

Chapter 4

God and Country

When we send our sons and daughters off to war, we take comfort in the consolation that they will not go alone.

When asked why they serve, most respond "God and Country". There is no higher calling than the compelling inspiration from God and "Uncle Sam".

We've been told there are no atheists in fox holes.

Nana's poems are generally written in iambic pentameter format. Almost every poem that Nana pens is a "country song" just waiting to happen. Add a bridge and chorus and a song is born. Nana feels that songs can be more stirring than poems. Nobody ever tapped a toe to a poem. I can't help but wonder what Lee Greenwood would do with her sentiments.

"Dog Tags and Crosses"

is my personal favorite

song title and lyric.

Dog Tags and Crosses

Verse 1

His country issued him dog tags
He wears them with pride;
Metal symbols of service
'Round his neck, tucked inside,
Engraved are his birthdate,
Social number and name,
His blood type and religion,
A pair of tags, both the same.

Verse 2

His mother gave him a silver cross
He wears it with pride;
A sterling symbol of faith
'Round his neck, tucked inside
Engraved it reads "all my love,
May God go with you".
She knows he won't walk alone
She prays God brings him through.

Chorus

Dog tags and crosses mingle close to his heart
Signs of all that is sacred and right
Dog tags and crosses reminding him daily
God and country's the reason he fights.

Verse 3
Tempered symbols of service
Worn for all men to see,
Reflecting his convictions
And what he believes.
He fights for justice and freedom
Prays for unity and peace.
He'll wear his dog tags and cross
'Till all oppression has ceased.

Bridge
With his country behind him
He knows he's never on his own
And with God at his side,
He never marches alone.

Tag
Dog tags and crosses
Reminding him daily
God and country's the reason he fights.

© Carol Wood aka Platoon Nana

Chapter 5

The Going Away Party

Larissa had received her departure date for Boot Camp. Now it's time to plan the party. Rather than bore you with my blurred vision of that day, you can see it through the eyes of a seven-year-old girl. Larissa's cousin from Long Island vividly reflects on that day. Let me share the essay that was written by my niece, Briana. That's Brian with an A. It was an honor to have a girl named after me. I joke about it all the time, but I am extremely honored. She is amazing. Wise beyond her years just like her uncle. Ha-ha!

This essay was written four years later for a school project. Briana was recollecting the party when she was only seven years old. Hers was the only composition that made her teacher cry. I was floored when my brother Dan called and read it to me.

This is Briana's perspective... Interesting how the kids are affected.

Through The Eyes of a Child...

Briana Wood   6/1/15

Writing   Personal Narrative

<u>Larissa's Goodbye Party</u>

One gorgeous June day in Syracuse, NY, I was at my Uncle Brian's, beautiful house for my cousin, Larissa's goodbye party. She was going into the Army. Larissa is very special to me. We have been an unstoppable team since I was born 7 years ago. Larissa and I were hanging out, watching TV and listening to music while we were waiting for the rest of the family to join us. Ding-dong!

Oh! It's our cousins, Cory, Kyle and baby Cole along with Aunt Linda and Uncle Dave. Following is Larissa's brother Michael and his girlfriend Jill. Soon, everyone else was there. Since the weather was so lovely, my cousins and I were playing outside. The scent of barbeque lingered in the air. Outside, my older cousins and I were being chased by little Cole. Of course, we ran very slowly and let him catch us. At the same time, Larissa and I were caught by him. I remember the exact moment like it was yesterday. She suddenly became overwhelmed with emotion.

Larissa was crying. "Wow, I love you guys so much, I am going to miss you like crazy." She said this with a look on her face like she was a sad puppy in the window.

We all agreed with her and joined in on a group hug. *We will miss each other like crazy.* I thought during the hug. *I miss her already.*

"Dinner is ready" shouted Uncle Brian from the deck.

As soon as that was said, we ran in the house like cheetahs. The barbeque food tasted better than it smelled (which was hard to believe because it smelled like heaven). My Uncle Brian grilled hamburgers and hotdogs. We all chipped in for pizza from our favorite pizza parlor in Syracuse, Twin Trees. It was delicious.

On top of that, they prepared a salad with – my favorite-croutons! All the food was delicious.

Out of nowhere we heard, "bawoon, bawoon." "Hey look, Cole wants a balloon" Michael said.

As was expected, Michael grabbed a blue balloon and gave it to Cole. Unexpectedly, he grabbed a red one for himself. My whole family gathered around the fireplace and watched as Michael ripped the string off the balloon. *What is he about to do*, I thought? He somehow managed to take the tie out of the balloon. He started sucking the helium out of it! He took the balloon out of his mouth and started speaking. His voice was so squeaky and cute! I loved it! It was really funny! My cousin Kyle described it as a chipmunk voice. *I love moments like this. Moments were everyone is laughing. I thought to myself, I wish this moment would last forever.*

Soon, the laughter came to a halt and down came the water-works. My family was scared, Larissa was scared, I was scared. *What if something happens to her*? That same thought kept haunting me. I finally said something.

"Larissa, you can't go!"

As I said that, I realized that Larissa is so strong and can conquer anything she sets her mind too. I figured I was just going to miss her. I concluded my sentence with,

"I am going to miss you so much."

"I am going to miss you too," She started, "But, I'm bringing you with me."

"What do you mean?" I asked confused.

"You will be right here" Larissa patted her heart.

"I'll bring you every step of the way." She finished.

I leaped into her arms, and we stayed that way for a while.

"I love you Breezy." She said.

"I love you more, Rissy." I replied.

Larissa was feeling very happy because she was with everyone that she loved. On the other hand, she was nervous because she knew she wasn't going to see her loved ones for a while and was off to basic training. My Uncle Brian was a little uneasy - looking himself. He was sad, nervous, and proud all at the same time. He was sad and nervous because his little girl was leaving to go into the army. He was proud because his baby is serving our country. I was proud as well.

Although we were "broken" into tears, my relationship with Larissa will never be broken. We were very upset that we wouldn't see each other for, possibly years, but we were still that unstoppable team that we were and always will be until the end.

I hope you enjoyed Briana's story. On an interesting note, I hadn't read Briana's account for several years. While proofreading the book I realized how similarly we write. Either I write like an 11-year-old girl or she writes like a 50-year-old man. Let's go with the latter.

On a more serious note, the first words that come to most people's minds in a similar situation are proud, scared, sad and nervous; the very same adjectives Briana and I used.

What better sentiments to impart to an 18-year-old embarking on a new and exciting journey

What To Give and Keep

To your country give allegiance;
Serve with dignity and pride.
Defend our precious freedoms,
Setting prejudice aside.

To your parents give great honor;
God demands it in his word.
"That your days upon the Earth may be long"
It's a commandment we've all heard.

To the one to whom you make the vow;
To love, honor and obey.
Give undying love and fidelity
Every hour of every day.

To your children give protection;
May they never taste of fear.
Shower them with gifts of praise,
They believe the words they hear.

To your friends the greatest gift you give
Is the gift of loyalty.
Keep a confidence - prove trustworthy;
Be the best friend you can be.

To yourself be true, never compromise;
Set high and lofty goals.
Keep the two most precious gifts you have,
Never lose your mind or soul.

© Carol Wood

Chapter 6

MEPS - Reality Sets In

MEPS is the Acronym for Military Entrance Processing Station.

No more vacations. The party's over! Talk about a roller coaster ride. Today we are scheduled to watch Larissa pledge her oath at the New York Air National Guard 174th attack wing in Syracuse NY.

From the gate, it's intimidating. Military police are armed with M-16 rifles. It's unsettling to know that before long my daughter will be issued one.

This was a day of mixed emotions. This is it! There's no turning back! This was the day we learned that only one percent of our population serve in the military.

We witnessed a group of young men and women including Larissa pledge an oath to their country. They will train with the elite. They will now serve The United States Army. Wow! You walk away numb. Once again, very proud, but numb.

I saw the fear in Larissa's eyes, the fear of the unknown. Basic training is real. Boot camp and drill sergeants are just around the corner.

Nevertheless, at the same time, she knew she was ready. She will serve her country, travel the world and experience life.

In the induction area there is a prominent display of literature. Nana gathered a handful of brochures. The one that struck her deepest alluded to the alarming rate of suicide. A seed was planted.

The new recruits were ordered to report to a hotel at carrier circle where Larissa and her fellow soldiers were being processed. She shared a room with someone she had never met until that evening. Think about that alone. What an uncomfortable feeling that must have been.

Their plane was scheduled to depart the next morning. We met Larissa at the airport for that final departure. The tsunami of tears that ensued could have swept her away more swiftly than the plane she bordered for Missouri.

My father had typed and laminated a poem that my mother penned for Larissa which she tucked in her backpack.

You Will Not Go Alone

Tho' your father and your mother
Can no longer hold your hand,
You will not travel by yourself
Whether air or sea or land.

You'll bid your family and your friends
A fond but sad farewell,
But you won't travel by yourself
You know it all too well.

We'll miss your smile and laughter,
We can't bear to see you go,
But you won't travel by yourself
That's one thing we all know.

Tho' the One who walks beside you
May not be seen nor heard,
You will not travel by yourself
He's given you, His word.

We'll shed our tears, we'll count the days
Until you come back home,
Our only solace is God's promise,
You will not go alone.

© Carol Wood

Chapter 7

Dreaded Boot Camp

It's May 16, 2011. Larissa's off to Fort Leonard Wood, Missouri. We've all heard about boot camp. We've seen it in the Movies. Few of us, myself included, have experienced boot camp first hand. Ten long and arduous weeks for the soldiers. Ten long and unsettling weeks for families.

We all waited anxiously for that first phone call letting us know she arrived. We waited, and waited and waited for the phone to ring. Let me tell you, that anxiously awaited phone call is not a long call. They basically let you know they've arrived safely and will contact you sometime in the near future. Larissa asked me to let everyone know she was safe and that she loves me. Click! END OF CALL.

This is real! Reality 101.

The next two weeks were a complete blur. I tried to go about my daily business. I showed up at work, pretended to go about my daily routine and continued my daily activities. I bragged about Larissa to anyone who would listen.

In addition to my concern for Larissa, I was extremely worried about her nana as well. At least I was able to sleep at night. Poor mom couldn't.

She was worried and felt guilty because she was sleeping in a comfortable bed and feared Larissa wasn't sleeping at all. My dad was our ROCK! Without his calm demeanor and wisdom, we would have all cracked. While we continue to live as normally as possible, Something's Missing.

About two weeks had passed. I went to the mailbox like any other day, and there it was; the coolest little letter I've ever received. Inside was a small yellow government issue paper with short lines, laced with Larissa's DNA and the teeny, tiniest handwriting I have ever seen. On the outside of the folded message she wrote, Padre. That was the name that I was given by Larissa from her high school Spanish class. She loved that class and adored and respected her teacher. I cherish the Spanish twist on father. She's Pooh-Bear and I'm Padre. I carried that tiny, little yellow letter in my wallet until it nearly disintegrated.

My Mother wrote Larissa every day with words of encouragement and crafted a new poem weekly for the platoon. Larissa would read the poems to friends and bunk mates. It wasn't long after, Larissa messaged Nana that not all of the soldiers received mail. It broke Nana's heart. She asked for names and began sending additional letters and poems, so they too received something at mail call.

Larissa's compassion made us proud. I was equally proud to have a mother that would take the time to write letters and poems to soldiers she had never met.

Perhaps one of the best things that came from this journey was the coveted name bequeathed to my mother. She was affectionately dubbed "Platoon Nana " by Larissa's boot camp platoon; a term of endearment she cherishes to this day.

Back in Syracuse our family is safe at home going about our daily routines. Our conversations and thoughts revolve around our darling soldier girl...Something's Missing!

Back at the barracks my soldier girl writes to tell us how painful the blisters were on her feet. She asked us to send bandages for her and her bunk mates. Larissa was warned prior to boot camp of the brutal abuse that feet take from the long hikes in military boots. She wasn't complaining, merely acknowledging the stark reality. In addition to the care package for their feet, and at the expense of Larissa's TI (Training Instructor), Nana's prescription included a heavy dose of levity.

Pretty Little Feet

I'm sorry you have blisters
From your long and grueling walks.
I think it's time that your TI
And Nana has a talk.

I hope your pretty little feet
Begin to heal real fast.
I wish that I was there
To boot your TI in the _ _ _ (butt)!

TI (Training Instructor)
© Carol Wood

37

What better place to interject some humor and an admonition from nana

Most fledgling soldiers are under the legal drinking age. That's reassuring! Armed with the rational that if they are old enough to serve, they are old enough to drink.

Nana offers a cautionary word.

Glasses vs. Glasses

They say rose colored glasses
Will obscure reality,
That when the world looks rosy pink
It's la-la land you see.

There are glasses far more skewed
Through which to view the world.
Nana says shot glasses
Blur more lines for guys and girls.

© Carol Wood

We were horrified to learn that Larissa won a contest for remaining the longest in the treacherous gas chamber exercise. Yes, a gas chamber is required in order to complete boot camp training and this "little nut" won. We think she lost. Lol

Ten long weeks have finally passed. Our Soldier Girl has survived. Our family has survived. With the end of boot camp comes a great relief, and yet there remains a void. Something's Missing!

Chapter 8

Platoon Nana's in The Camp

Yup it's time! We hope the worst is over. Boot camp has ended and families that are lucky enough to attend will celebrate a proud day at the graduation in Fort Leonard Wood, Missouri. Nana and I have already booked our flights for the graduation ceremony.

It was comical. On graduation day, Larissa's platoon buddies and Nana's pen pals asked how they would recognize Platoon Nana. Riss replied simply, "It'll be easy, just look for the Diva."

Platoon Nana is in the camp and excited to meet her pen pals and greet the fellow soldiers who had accompanied Larissa on this leg of her journey.

I've never been more excited than to see Larissa and meet her new friends. I was happy to share the day with Larissa's grandmother who offered words of encouragement and brought small tokens of appreciation.

Platoon Nana wasn't hard to spot. She arrived in a bright chartreuse green blouse; not a hair out place and her makeup was flawless. She was ready to meet her new pen pals.

It was us who had a hard time spotting our soldier girl. Riss was in formation with hundreds of other soldiers wearing identical uniforms. She was wearing the exact same glasses that every soldier that failed the eye exam was issued. She was sporting large black, by no means trendy, eyewear that she referred to as "birth control" glasses.

I'm sure you figured it out. We spotted her. It's amazing how your own child stands out in a crowd. We were full of pride and joy, yet to see her up close was sad. Her cute little nose was beet red and her ears were brown and peeling from sunburn. Her platoon had been training in scorching heat during the hottest summer on record. During these brutal conditions our fledgling soldiers never complained.

The soldiers conducted a beautiful, memorable ceremony for parents and family members. The presentation included a larger-than-life video documenting their competitions, drills and classes. We all had a front row seat to their journey and accomplishments.

To make our day even more special, Larissa was one of the few graduates to address the assembly. Normally a shy girl, Riss was now speaking in front of hundreds. She participated in competitions that included grueling training exercises that were magnified on the big screen. I was beaming with pride from ear to ear. Toby Keith's "American Soldier" was the perfect song choice for the stirring background music. The US military did its job. Our sons and daughters are now military grade soldiers ready for the next endeavor or encounter.

After 10 weeks of rigorous basic training in the hottest summer on record, our darling soldier girl was swept off to missile training camp in Fort Sill, Oklahoma. She was unable to return home and reconnect with those who could not attend the graduation ceremony. Something's Missing!!

Larissa

A good time to share two versions of Nana's "Hey Guys"

Hey Guys

Hey guys, I think you're lucky
To be serving with my "Riss"
I know she'll always have your back,
She's tough - depend on this.

I'm sure she's just as lucky
To be serving with you too.
I know you'll watch her back as well
'Cause that's what soldiers do.

You'll make good friends
and forge strong bonds,
Create a "unit" that's for sure!
The relationship that soldiers build
Are ones that will endure.

© Carol Wood

Hey Guys - Version 2

Hey guys, look out for my soldier girl
Help make her army tough,
Just promise you won't teach her
How to 'whiz' while standing up.

© Carol Wood

Chapter 9
Artillery Training

Larissa arrives at Fort Sill for ten more grueling weeks of training in the sweltering heat. Countless hours of classroom study are required to complete her missile defense training that is deemed necessary for the next endeavor. At the end of the ten weeks, she will have earned a short five-day visit home.

  I booked a flight to Fort Sill, Oklahoma where I arranged to stay at an IHG army hotel on the base. I was intent on learning more about military life. I witnessed firsthand a soldier's total commitment and relinquishment of all power and choice.

  My beautiful soldier girl's skin was riddled with a

"pox like" reaction to an anthrax shot. The whole side of her back and shoulder was broken out from the vaccine. How sobering and horrific is the thought that our sons and daughters are threatened with, and subject to, the real possibility of chemical warfare. This was one the most bothersome events of the journey.

On a brighter note, Larissa sat with me to watch one of my favorite movies that I was confident she would like. We watched "Josey Wales" starring Clint Eastwood. I think she actually liked it. Well, at least she said she did. Lol

The Josey Wales connection led us to one of the most memorable discoveries of the visit. We learn that Geronimo and his family were buried somewhere on the base. Larissa and I drove to the hallowed grounds and prayed at the grave site of this brave warrior. Standing in this sacred place was humbling and changed my life. I realized that history must never be erased or forgotten and that we must learn from the past in order to improve our future.

The following day Riss and I returned to Syracuse. There was so much catching up to do. She missed so many meaningful events. She missed Father's Day, Mother's Day, birthdays, anniversaries and the birth of her first nephew Vincent.

After five short days with family and friends, Larissa prepared for the next leg of her journey; a one-year deployment to South Korea. We are once again saying goodbyes at the airport. Our brave, adventurous eighteen-year-old soldier is flying alone to reconnect with her platoon. I can't imagine, at eighteen, flying to another continent by myself. This is no family vacation.

Riss during classroom training. The sergeant patch is another example of what the mind can conceive and believe it will achieve. She was a private first class at the time, wearing a temporary patch.

Larissa continued to send teeny, tiny yellow notes back home. She thanked Nana for all of the poems and confessed that if she had to choose her favorite, it would be "My Wish"

Larissa's Personal Favorite

My Wish

I wish that I could march with you
And carry half your load
I ache to cool you when it's hot,
And warm you when you're cold.

I long to make the trip with you
And hold your hand each step.
I'd like to send a gentle breeze,
That dries you when you're wet.

I'd like to keep you from all harm,
Protect you from all foes.
My prayer for you is that you're safe,
No matter where you go.

I want you to experience pride
That comes from serving others.
I hope you know how proud we are
Your friends, your dad, your mother.

But most of all I wish that you
Return back home to stay;
And wisely use the lessons
That you've learned along the way.

© Carol Wood

Chapter 10

The DMZ - Demilitarization Zone

This zone is a stretch of no man's land on the northern border of South Korea.

Larissa is fully trained to operate the avenger, a mobile ground to air missile defense system. Her job is to protect South Korea from a North Korean invasion. The thought is terrifying, yet without pause or hesitation she soldiers on.

For a full year my darling soldier girl lives and trains in the fields of South Korea. The region is notorious for blazing hot summers and bone chilling winters. Soldiers rotate one week, every month camping outdoors while protecting the country's border. Ask any Korean war veteran about the conditions. Most will recollect the brutal winters and fear of freezing to death.

Larissa's platoon was able to "escape" from base periodically. She relayed a touching and eventful day in South Korea. Larissa and her fellow soldiers posed a challenge to "high five" as many Korean nationals as possible.

The challenge was met by South Koreans laughing and returning the "high fives". To Larissa, if no one else, the exercise affirmed Nana's contention and song lyrics that "We're More Alike Than Not"

Excerpt from the song "We're More Alike Than Not"

CHORUS

All our tears flow colorless
The blood we shed runs red.
We're not so very different
When all is done and said.
We teach our precious children
The very lessons we've been taught.
When the sun goes down
and the moon comes up
We're more alike than not.

© Carol Wood

Back home, Platoon Nana continues to write. Poems and songs are flooding her mind. She writes and writes and writes. She learned that due to PTSD and separation anxiety the suicide rate is growing. Platoon Nana realizes that the suicide ratio is higher in our military, resulting in more than twenty suicides a day.

The poem that Nana wrote with the greatest passion is "Hold on Another Day." She considers it her most compassionate poem "God Only Knows"

If Nana could be remembered for only one poem, it would be "Hold on Another Day"

(Suicide Prevention)

Hold On Another Day

At times the hopeless feeling
May seem more than you can bear,
In the darkness of your anguish
You can't see the ones who care.

Look for that ray of sunlight,
Imagine what your mother would say.
You know how she would plead
That you hold on another day.

You're not alone - though it feels that way,
Your despair just clouds the face
Of those who truly love you
And would gladly take your place.

Look through the clouds and search your heart
Imagine what your friends would say.
You know they would encourage you
To hold on another day.

Know if you choose to end your pain,
Another's pain will just begin.
The thoughts not meant to bring you guilt,
Just the will to live again.

The rocks and mountains would cry out,
The universe would say
How much you truly matter,
So, Hold on Another Day.

© Carol Wood

Chapter 11

Fort Hood

Larissa's one year tour of duty has ended and she is flown back to her new home base where she will continue her training at Fort Hood in Killeen, Texas.

Seems like strange timing, however I want to pause for a moment to thank you for staying on this roller coaster ride with me. Let's take a moment to coast, catch our breath and reflect.

I realize this is a personal journey, yet we all share similar emotions. I believe we can all agree that it's incumbent upon us to remind the 99% of the commitment and sacrifice of the mere 1% who serve.

We are two thirds of the way through this book. By now you probably believe my assertion that I am not a "writer." Hopefully, you also realize how important it is to me to release these thoughts into the universe.

So, back to my story and to one of the most impactful events that occurred during Larissa's stint at Fort Hood. Sadly, a fellow soldier girl was diagnosed with cancer and would require treatments a great distance from the base.

The young soldier was instructed to select the "battle buddy" of her choice to accompany her on the course of treatment. Chelsea chose Larissa. What an honor!

She and Larissa became fast friends and traveled together to Austin, Texas. After Chelsea's daily treatments at a nearby hospital, Larissa would spend her evenings with family members of other patients at The Fisher House. Fisher House assists thousands of families with free lodging in close proximity to Veteran hospitals. What a worthy organization to support.

Sadly, due to chemotherapy, her friend had to shave her head. In a gesture of solidarity, my darling soldier girl shaved her head as well; a stellar example of loyalty and comradery. I've never been prouder!

In recognition of their shared experience,

Nana penned a poem "Bald Buddies" for Chelsea and Larissa.

Rather than share their very personal poem, I have included the encouragement and consolation that Nana offers breast cancer survivors.

Pink Ribbons

Pink Ribbons weave a winding path
No woman wants to take,
But with love, support and company
It's a journey you can make.

Pink ribbons take their twists and turns
Where they lead God only knows.
For the legion of survivors,
Ribbons form a pretty bow.

© Carol Wood

Chapter 12

Two Years Have Passed

Finally, Larissa is long overdue for a two week visit home; a time to see friends and family and share her life's experiences.

Her nephew Vincent is now two years old. She had been unable to hold him or celebrate his first two birthdays. She has now missed more than one easter, thanksgiving and Christmas celebration with family and friends. Nothing's the same... Something's Missing.

While Larissa's been away, we have been attending military functions and fundraisers. Nana is fast becoming armed with ammunition and inspiration for more poems and lyrics.

We had been working on a song that Platoon Nana wrote for Riss. We couldn't wait to share it with my "Pooh Bear." This is the poem version of "You Don't March Alone." It was also produced as a song to which Nana added a chorus and tag. In it, Nana chronicles signs in nature that correlate to our thoughts and emotions.

Universal signs to Riss that she is not alone. My father called them "God Winks."

Two weeks fly by and we're back to the airport to say our goodbyes once again. My darling soldier girl is headed back to Texas to her home base at Fort Hood.

© Carol Wood

A heartfelt sentiment that could go to every soldier from any parent, grandparent, significant other, spouse, or child.

You Don't March Alone

At first the hint of a new day,
The rising sun comes breaking through;
It's warmth and light reminders
That I'm smiling down on you.

Then comes a sweet and welcome rain,
That's sent to gently cool your face;
It's a symbol of my teardrops,
If I could, I'd take your place.

At night God scatters all the stars
That blink to tell you that I'm there;
Through them, I watch you every night,
You are always in my prayers.

So, watch and listen carefully,
Look all around and you will see;
'God winks and sweet reminders
That you're never far from me.

Throughout this awesome universe,
Signs you're never on your own,
All nature chimes in unison
Soldier, You Don't March Alone.

© Carol Wood

Chapter 13

Off to Kuwait - Fox Treats

Platoon Nana and Padre are still working on songs, poems and projects that shine a light on our military. Our soldier girl receives her orders for her second one-year deployment to Kuwait where she will work on the patriot missile program. She will put her skills and training into practice.

Her platoon is in charge of the Patriot missile program that was designed to intercept missiles that may be fired at our troops in Afghanistan. It is an extraordinarily sophisticated piece of equipment requiring highly trained military personnel to maneuver and operate.

A lover of nature and adventure, Larissa elected

to sleep out under the stars rather than in the barracks. In the field she encountered an unlikely "friend". On the first evening, she was awakened to find a little fennec fox, with cartoon-like ears, sniffing her head. The following night the little rascal nudged her boot to announce his arrival. He returned nightly to greet her and be rewarded with "bribes" of food. Her new friend deserved a name. So, Riss dubbed him Todd from a Disney character in the movie "The Fox and The Hound."

A friend heard about Todd and "googled" the fact that foxes like dog treats. Her friend's next care package from home included a box of treats that she gifted Riss.

Despite warnings of the threat of scorpions and deadly snakes in the desert, they rendezvoused nightly. Todd promptly buried the "American" treats in the Kuwait desert. Riss and Todd continued to share the shenanigans until she was ordered to her new post as sergeant of the guard.

Wouldn't you know, Platoon Nana finds inspiration in the strangest places. After all, when in imminent danger, where do soldiers retreat? FOXHOLES!

Enter Todd, the adorable little military fox. Before long Nana found an illustrator to "flesh out" the comical critter. Todd became the inspiration for "Art Tillery" Art now needs a "soldier girl" counterpart. So…. enter Miss L

(L for Larissa).

Nana's done it again. Her unique play on words catapulted two military terms (artillery & missile) into two full blown cartoon characters…" Sgt. Art Tillery" & "Pvt. Miss L."

Larissa continues to work hard. She never complains! God, how we miss her.

During that long year, we are adapting, but something's still missing! It's 120 degrees in the desert, and we are at home enjoying our air conditioning.

There were times we feared the anxiety would kill Nana. Fortunately, inhaling and exhaling are involuntary.

We continue to coast through our daily activities. Platoon Nana continues to write. She writes and writes and writes. Inspiration is coursing through her veins and onto paper, demonstrating that the pen is indeed mightier than the sword. She continues to write about conditions reserved for those who serve. Weighing most heavily on her mind and heart is the escalating rate of suicide in the military. In the meantime, a tragedy strikes close to home. A friend's son who was a master chef in Syracuse had committed suicide. Nana was inspired to write the poem "God Only Knows" for the mother of the young man.

Mom shared the poem with others. Eventually it was forwarded to an army chaplain in Ohio. Chaplain Bev sent the poem to families of suicide victims. The poem has been a source of comfort and consolation to many who have endured the unimaginable pain of loss due to suicide. Nana counts the notes and letters of appreciation as her most treasured correspondence.

One's first response to the horrific notification of suicide can be summed up in one word. Why?? We don't know why. We can't provide the answer that God Only Knows.

God Only Knows

God only knows the frailty of man;
How much each one can take,
And He alone can understand,
What makes one of His children break.

We cannot comprehend how one
We love would choose to leave.
Trust God to wipe away your tears,
Through your pain, strive to believe.

Don't blame yourself, or ask "what if."
Cherish memories you hold dear,
If love alone had been enough,
Then they would still be here.

They could not find the peace they sought
Anywhere this side of Heaven,
So, they fell into the only arms
That could hold them twenty-four, seven.

© Carol Wood

Chapter 14

America's Heroes Are Home

I was so thankful to be able to fly to Texas to welcome Larissa "home" and witness the homecoming of our troops. The platoon arrived in the middle of the night. The ceremony was moving and powerful.

At three o'clock in the morning, hundreds of friends and family gathered in the gymnasium. At the back entrance a fog machine created a mystical atmosphere through which over two hundred soldiers burst, single file, filling the auditorium. The floor rumbled as over 400 boots found their place in formation. Over the loudspeaker a deep voice echoed "America's Heroes Are Home." The crowd cheered, then the room went silent as flag bearers proceeded down the aisle. Every soldier stood at attention to salute the American flag. The ceremony ended with a thundering rendition of the National Anthem. No one knew if it was more pride or more relief that our soldiers were back on American soil.

After the ceremony I met Larissa's commanding officers and fellow soldiers. I was anxious to learn more about her friends and their families.

The following day, one of Larissa's friends called. She was at a car dealership. She was frustrated with the process and asked me to help negotiate the purchase of a new car. Business is business, and apparently not all dealerships demonstrate their appreciation of our armed forces.

Though old enough to serve, most of our soldiers lack experience in the art of negotiation. It was rewarding to be able to save her thousands of dollars over the course of the loan. I say this not to brag, but to challenge our generation to share their wealth of experience. I remember needing guidance; now it's my time to give back. Life comes full circle and the student becomes the teacher. Giving of one's time is perhaps the greatest gift of all.

One car fiasco after another. My darling soldier girl's car is no longer drivable. We needed to deal with her car that was left behind to rot in a storage shed. One year of storage fees down the toilet. The one hundred plus temperatures in Texas have taken a toll. We had the car towed to a nearby garage and wouldn't you know… yup! The law of attraction. Steve "Stone Cold" Austin was one of the mechanics. Well, it wasn't really Steve Austin the wrestler, but he sure did resemble him. Because it was a mini cooper built by BMW the repairs would have been prohibitive. Well, now we're back to the law of attraction. Stone Cold's wife always wanted a mini cooper. He made us a fair as-is offer and the rest is history. The car that was once our burden is now their blessing.

You're probably thinking enough already about cars. To put the car dynamic in perspective we have to recognize the importance of "wheels" to a young person. For most kids out of school a car is their single most important possession. It represents freedom. To a young soldier stationed overseas, their "symbol of freedom" must be sold or relegated to storage.

While in Kuwait Larissa was charged with the decision of whether to renew her contract with the military or return to civilian life. She crafted a plan that accomplished both. She chose to come home and reunite with her family and friends. At the same time, she elected to remain a "part time" soldier in the National Guard.

The lengthy reintegration process requires 4-6 weeks. It is necessary to complete a similar deactivation process for those who leave active duty. Ninety long days of anticipating her return. Something's still missing, but we stay the course.

Upon her return from active duty Riss "crashed" at Nana's. The stories they could tell. They laughed until they cried.

Riss thought they should take their act "on the road" or build a social media site. We could call it Funk N' Fun with Nana.

Larissa let no grass grow under her feet. In a span of just 3 years, she earned her dental assistant license and acquired a commercial driver's license to drive a school bus. While on the subject of licenses, she got her motorcycle license as well. Not good news for Nana and Padre. I collect antiques and she collected licenses.

The curse of a worldwide pandemic placed her on

a new path. She was called to serve once again and was offered an opportunity to work full time in the National Guard. She has since been married, earned her sergeant stripes and transferred to Schenectady, NY.

This roller coaster ride has many twists, turns and loops. You can hear the clicking of the track and feel the jerking motion that ushers you to the top. Without warning or time to catch your breath, a G-force gravity sends you plummeting back toward earth. Thankfully, every one that boarded our roller coaster returned safely.

Our family's journey has been an adventure full of twists and turns that ultimately resulted in a great learning experience.

Chapter 15

Not All Returned

Not Every Soldier Survived
Not Every Hero Returned

Sadly, not every family gets to celebrate the homecoming ceremony. We met and empathized with so many gold star mothers and fathers. Our greatest inspiration comes from the mothers who dress in white and wear the gold star.

We commiserate with the gold star fathers who stand beside them. Mothers and fathers whose mission becomes honoring and remembering the sons and daughters who never returned. They have paid the ultimate price for the cost of war. I confess that in the small recesses of my mind, I am thankful not to be counted among them.

For me, the most heart wrenching and heartwarming moments of every Veteran's Day and armed services observance is the participation and contribution of the Gold Star Mothers. My mother's inspiration for this poem came from the first gold star mother she met.

A Tribute to Gold Star Families

Will and Marcia, we shall
never forget the impact you have
had on our hearts and lives.

In Memory of
Lt. Patrick K. Connor US Navy

Let This Cup Pass from Me

A Gold Star Mother's Prayer

You know I love my country Lord
I pray for peace and unity,
But not my son or daughter God
Let this cup pass from me.

I know that freedoms bought with blood
All men are not born free.
I've seen the price that some have paid,
But, let this cup pass from me.

We beam with pride when our children stand
Against persecution and tyranny,
And though you know how proud I am
Let this cup pass from me.

But should I taste the bitter cup
I pray on bended knee that
I bear the loss and endure the pain
With grace and serenity.

And while these earthly tears shall flow
Remind me now and then;
They're gone for just one tour of duty
And we will meet again.

© Carol Wood

Chorus and tag
from the heart-rending song

His Brother's Carried His Body

CHORUS

His brother's carried his body,
all broken and bloody
Off a battlefield stained with his blood
He heard his mother's voice crying,
like she knew he was dying
As angels ushered his spirit toward God.

TAG

He ain't heavy, he's my brother
Kept running through their minds
While in their heads a voice was ringing
Leave no man behind.

© Carol Wood

Chapter 16

Never Quit

The Admonition of Muhammed Ali

I almost quit writing this book a dozen times, but I couldn't live with the label "quitter". Looking back, I experienced many highs and lows on the roller coaster. I felt like I was wasting my time. "I am not a writer. No one wants to hear my story." I was reminded of a conversation that I had with Dr. Ferdie Pacheco (Mohammed Ali's fight doctor).

Years ago, I published the art of Dr. Pacheco. I will never forget meeting him in his Miami home. In his deep, raspy, unmistakable commentator voice he reiterated what Muhammed Ali always said, "Never Quit, Never Quit." My Parents never quit; Larissa never quit! My son Mike never quit. I wasn't going to be the first in my family to quit.

Our Vets Never Quit.

Vets Continue to Serve

It's in their blood, in their DNA
Men and women wired to serve;
The first to answer their country's call
Born with grit, brave hearts and nerve.

It's not surprising when their service ends
And our Veterans return
That they look for ways to continue to serve
And apply the skills they've learned.

They're fueled by a fire of comradery,
They're trained to function as a team
They reintegrate into society
And perpetuate the American dream.

© Carol Wood

Chapter 17

Road to the Honor Guard

Many evenings after dinner, Larissa and Nana weighed Riss's options for the future. Larissa wasn't home long when she knew that service in the honor guard would be included.

Nana had a bird's eye view of the preparation that Riss devoted to each and every service. She watched as Riss painstakingly positioned and repositioned every medal and bar on her meticulously clean midnight blue jacket. Shoes were polished to a patent leather luster. The crease in her contrasting blue pants was straight and single. When she tucked her neatly wrapped bun under her hat, she looked like a recruitment poster for the United States Army.

She explained to Nana how the flags were neatly folded and presented to the families. Nana knew from attending military funerals what was to come; a bugler pointed his shiny brass horn toward Heaven and began to play taps, the gut-wrenching melody that brings everyone in the service to tears. What a beautiful contribution and fitting ending to a fond farewell. It would impossible to quantify the depth and breadth of pride I feel as a father.

A final tribute to every Veteran who leaves this world for the next

Eternal Thanks

You've made your final march
And you fought your final war.
A bright and peaceful place awaits
At the end of your last tour.

On your final tour of duty
You leave this world for the next.
Where there's no war or casualties
Just perfect peace and rest.

All earthly pain and sorrow past
On gossamer wings you leave.
Your journey has not ended
It has just begun, BELIEVE!

We're told that we take nothing
When we leave this world behind
Not true; you take Eternal Thanks
Today and for all time.

© Carol Wood

Chapter 18

Freedom To Think - Democracy

Some nations are thousands of years old and steeped in principles of dictatorship; Marxism, socialism, totalitarianism and communism. These are the nations people seek to escape. America is a young country founded on the principles of five freedoms; freedom of speech, religion, press, assembly and the right to petition the government. We are the country with the highest immigration population in the world. Most "ISM'S " stifle creative thinking. Capitalism gives it free reign.

One of our greatest freedoms is the freedom to think. Why do other countries steal our intellectual properties, our ideas, our concepts and our patents? Why is it that their greatest talent is the ability to reverse engineer. The answer is simple.

They are NOT free to think!

Chapter 19

Freedom Isn't Free

Freedom comes at an enormous price. How do we measure the cost of war? Is it by the cost of planes, helicopters, tanks, ships, submarines, missiles, drones and artillery? Who pays for the cost of war? Is it the taxpayer, the government? The ultimate price is paid by every man and woman who ever wore a military uniform. Freedom comes at a great loss. Freedom comes at an enormous cost.

Americans measure the cost of war...

Drop,
by Drop,
by Drop.

Every drop...a jewel in the crown of freedom.
    Every drop...a nail in the coffin of oppression.

© Carol Wood

Chapter 20

The Debt We Can Never Repay

How can we fully express the gratitude we owe our Vietnam War Veterans who thanklessly served in that horrific war. They served because their country called and were harshly judged as if it was a choice.

Every annual Veteran's Day observance is structured around a theme. The year that the program honored the Vietnam War Veterans proved to be a challenge for platoon nana. That was the war of her generation. How would she reconcile the pride she shared for friends, family and classmates who served, with the frustration she felt toward those who shunned them.

The Result of Nana's Internal Dialogue and Mixed Emotions

The Debt We Can Never Repay

In Honor of Vietnam Vets

Through the jungles of Vietnam
You held our banner high
You trudged through muddy waters
You fought, you bled, you died.

The choice to fight, not yours to make
You'd heed your country's call
You served with honor and loyalty
You watched your comrades fall.

Over fifty-eight thousand Americans died
Fifty-eight thousand mothers wept
Nearly ten percent of Americans served
Ninety percent of Americans slept.

In return for sleeping in jungles
And for fighting the Viet Cong
You received no hero's welcome
You were scorned and spit upon

The remnant of a band of warriors
Bearing scars until this day
Fifty years later we're still reminded
Of a debt we can never repay.

© Carol Wood

Chapter 21

Behold The Freedom Tower

Nothing ignites the spirit of our defenders more than a war waged on our homeland.

9-11 stirred a swell of emotions and a pitch of patriotism never before experienced in American history. The bombing of the twin towers represented the first invasion from a foreign country on American soil. America's response was swift and furious. Al-Qaeda was in the cross hairs of a battle that would not end for twenty years.

Young Americans rallied, resulting in the biggest boon in recruitment since WW II. Larissa was only 9 years old when the towers fell. I believe many of her generation waited "on deck" to be eligible to bear arms.

I doubt there lives an American who doesn't remember where they were when the twin towers fell. Nana was in the bedroom watching tv when the horrific news bulletin aired. She watched in disbelief as the second plane hit the second tower.

"Freedom Tower" Holds a Special Place In Platoon Nana's Heart

Freedom Tower

America will never forget
The morning of Nine Eleven,
When from the ashes, a cloud of smoke
Rose all the way to Heaven.

A legion of responders streamed
Where angels fear to tread;
A tomb of broken humanity
Like the sea giving up it's dead.

Three thousand souls and two towers fell
'Midst an inferno of airplane fuel.
Thru flames resilient hearts were tempered.
In the crucible, resolve just grew.

Countless names inscribed in bronze,
Twin pools bathe sacred ground,
A stately tower rises higher
Than the two the terrorists downed.

Now on this hallowed memorial site,
Proof oppression holds no power,
Lift your eyes and search the heavens,
Behold the freedom tower.

© Carol Wood

Chapter 22

Thank You for Your Service

It is the Veterans who went before us that serve as an example and inspiration to every new generation of servicemen and women.

We sleep soundly at night because our military is second to none. Our wars are fought and won on the front lines. Our troops do battle on the ground in tanks, on foot, and in jeeps and combat vehicles. They fight in the air on planes, helicopters and fighter jets. They wage war on and under the sea, on aircraft carriers, ships and submarines.

As Americans we have much to be thankful for. Gratitude is counted among the most powerful of all human emotions. As children we are taught to always say "thank you". Motivational speakers encourage us to keep gratitude journals. To live in

Chapter 21

Behold The Freedom Tower

Nothing ignites the spirit of our defenders more than a war waged on our homeland.

9-11 stirred a swell of emotions and a pitch of patriotism never before experienced in American history. The bombing of the twin towers represented the first invasion from a foreign country on American soil. America's response was swift and furious. Al-Qaeda was in the cross hairs of a battle that would not end for twenty years.

Young Americans rallied, resulting in the biggest boon in recruitment since WW II. Larissa was only 9 years old when the towers fell. I believe many of her generation waited "on deck" to be eligible to bear arms.

   I doubt there lives an American who doesn't remember where they were when the twin towers fell. Nana was in the bedroom watching tv when the horrific news bulletin aired. She watched in disbelief as the second plane hit the second tower.

"Freedom Tower" Holds a Special Place In Platoon Nana's Heart

Freedom Tower

America will never forget
The morning of Nine Eleven,
When from the ashes, a cloud of smoke
Rose all the way to Heaven.

A legion of responders streamed
Where angels fear to tread;
A tomb of broken humanity
Like the sea giving up it's dead.

Three thousand souls and two towers fell
'Midst an inferno of airplane fuel.
Thru flames resilient hearts were tempered.
In the crucible, resolve just grew.

Countless names inscribed in bronze,
Twin pools bathe sacred ground,
A stately tower rises higher
Than the two the terrorists downed.

Now on this hallowed memorial site,
Proof oppression holds no power,
Lift your eyes and search the heavens,
Behold the freedom tower.

© Carol Wood

Chapter 22

Thank You for Your Service

It is the Veterans who went before us that serve as an example and inspiration to every new generation of servicemen and women.

We sleep soundly at night because our military is second to none. Our wars are fought and won on the front lines. Our troops do battle on the ground in tanks, on foot, and in jeeps and combat vehicles. They fight in the air on planes, helicopters and fighter jets. They wage war on and under the sea, on aircraft carriers, ships and submarines.

As Americans we have much to be thankful for. Gratitude is counted among the most powerful of all human emotions. As children we are taught to always say "thank you". Motivational speakers encourage us to keep gratitude journals. To live in a perpetual state of gratitude is life changing. When counting our blessings, we must include our armed forces; men and women who serve in the United States Army, Navy, Air Force, Marines and Coast Guard.

It is fitting that my story ends on a note of gratitude

Thank You for Your Service

Thank you for your service,
We'll sleep sound because you're there.
Someone needs to guard our freedoms,
And show the world we care.

Those of us with babes in arms
Or frail from golden age
Look to our bravest and our best
When there's a war to wage.

Many can't defend the cause
But we keep watch and pray.
We hold you close in thought and prayer,
We're grateful every day.

So, thank you for your service,
For standing in our place;
For serving with such dignity
Devotion, pride and grace.

© Carol Wood

God Bless The USA

Iris,

Thank you for your help and hosting our segment.

Strength Through Peace,

Brian K. Wood

Brian Wood - Author

Brian has two children and one grandson.

He was an entrepreneur from the age of five when he started selling seed packets, pewter crosses and "Dine-a-Mate" books door to door. Brian was twelve when he purchased his paper route. At fifteen he worked as a construction laborer and spent summers roofing houses. At just nineteen, Brian was self-employed and over the next 30 years built a premier antique, art and custom framing business. He was best known for his creative designs and meticulous craftsmanship. His unique shadow box projects brought him all-star and hall of fame athletes.

Brian was an agent to local, nationally and internationally acclaimed artists. He represented Dr. Ferdie Pacheco, an Emmy award winning sports commentator and "fight doctor" to Muhammed Ali.

Brian enjoys supporting local community programs, fundraisers and events. His participation in military programs directed him into product development and music production. Brian's hobbies included karate, fishing, skiing, baseball, hiking and coaching. His number one priority remains family and friends.

Carol Wood – Poet

Carol was married for 60 years. She is mother to 3 sons, 6 grandchildren and 1 great grandson. For 40 years she owned a fine antique, art and gift shop. Her hobbies consist of writing, decorating, landscaping and cooking. She is devoted to writing poems, songs, speeches and articles that shine a light on conditions reserved for our military. She continues to address a myriad of social conditions. Carol is a published poet and author of a children's book "Color Really Doesn't Matter". Her biography and philosophy are best summed up in a poem she penned forty years ago. It was reinterpreted in a painting by internationally acclaimed artist Gregory Perillo.

Iris, thank you!
Carol Wood

One in the Spirit

A boy, a girl it matters not
What shade or tinge of skin.
For all are colored in a hue,
Designed as seen by HIM.

A red, a yellow, black, a white
Has any one less merit,
No, not by One who made them
To be His, One in the Spirit.

© Carol Wood

Made in the USA
Monee, IL
23 June 2023